HOW TO IMPROVE

YOUR MIND

HOW TO IMPROVE YOUR MIND

BARUCH SPINOZA

With Biographical Notes
by DAGOBERT D. RUNES

THE WISDOM LIBRARY

A DIVISION OF

PHILOSOPHICAL LIBRARY

New York

The present edition is based on the text
De Intellectus Emendatione
translated from the Latin by R. H. M. ELWES

BARUCH SPINOZA

(*1632-1677*)

AMONG the hundreds of men of greater or less importance in the history of philosophy, Baruch Spinoza holds a unique position. Abhorred and reviled for more than a hundred years by the intellectual elite of Europe, this so-called wicked little atheist had, by the end of the eighteenth century, become a symbol of sanctity. Great men like Herder, Goethe and Lessing revered this strange man and his original ideas, and as the decades went by, the light of Baruch Spinoza's brilliant thought shone brighter and brighter.

No man can be fully understood without an adequate knowledge of his background; and if Spinoza seems to be an enigmatic figure, so were his epoch and his environment.

Spinoza was the descendant of a Jewish family which had been driven from Spain by the Inquisition, first to Portugal, then to Holland. The latter country offered only a partial refuge, for in the seventeenth century Holland had its own brands of religious and political persecution. Young Spinoza found little happiness in his step-mother's house in Amsterdam, and we hear of him as an adolescent frequently wandering away from the Spanish-speaking "ghetto," to mingle with his Christian neighbors. Amsterdam was at that time seething with Socinians, Quakers and other reformist sects, a situation which helped the young student of the Torah and the Talmud to approach scripture with an amazingly analytical and objective eye.

By his detached viewpoint, the young Spinoza brought to light indisputable discrepancies between various sections of the Canon, and confronted scholars with disturbing evidence that some of the traditionally ancient writings had been composed only a few hundred years B.C., and by entirely different hands than the orthodoxy alleged. This was the beginning of modern theological exegetics or Biblical criticism. The Jewish community of Amsterdam, most of whose members had suffered harrowing tortures at the hands of the Catholic Church, made desperate efforts to stop Spinoza from proselytizing among their people. What they especially feared was Spinoza's thesis that the laws of the Torah were state laws designed for the tribes of Israel, and therefore had no validity for Jews living in other states. If this interpretation was accepted, it would mean the dissolution of those religious ties by which the Torah had for thousands of years held together Jews scattered to the four corners of the earth. When pleas and threats proved to be of no avail, the twenty-four-year-old Spinoza was officially expelled from the Jewish community of Amsterdam. He spent the remainder of his life in other Dutch towns, mostly in and around The Hague.

Immediately after his excommunication, Spinoza had published in Spanish a pamphlet entitled *Apologia,* which explained his position. Until this day not one copy of the pamphlet has been discovered, though many years later, in the only book published during his lifetime, *The Theological Political Treatise,* he expounded his point of view in great detail. His main thesis is an appeal to reason, with the recommendation that the secular powers of the Church be curbed, so that every man might be granted full liberty of thought and speech.

In his philosophic method, Spinoza is a student of Déscartes, but in his findings he ranges far afield from the French mathematician. In his *Ethics,* which is designed after Euclid's *Geometry,* he begins with a number of what he considers irrefutable premises, on which he builds a system analyzing the nature of God and man in a purely scientific manner. He identifies God with creative nature, and with Substance. Mortal man knows only two attributes, the world of the body and the world of the mind; but God (or Substance) lives through infinite attributes, each of which in turn necessarily expresses eternal and infinite essentiality.

This majestic concept of our mind-body universe, as, so to speak, only a splinter in eternity, has had profound effect upon physicists and scholars from Leibniz to Einstein. Man himself, Spinoza reasons, is, like all things, a part, a mode, of created nature and must be taken as such and no more. Like other things, he is constantly in motion and has no free will of his own. He is filled with contradictory emotions of fear and hope, love and hate, pity and remorse. The only path to freedom from such an embattled existence is to be overwhelmed by an even greater emotion: the love of God, which is, indeed, the same as the love of man. Love of God is born out of deep understanding of the nature of the universe, and it is given only to those who perceive intellectually the self-identical order of ideas and things as attributes of the all-pervading One. Whoever gains this high intuition will become imbued with *amor dei intellectualis,* the rational love of God.

Thus the man who understands the order of creative nature, through his feeling of inner blessedness, sloughs off the disturbing passions of ambition, greed and lust, to enjoy the constant pleasure of fulfillment in having reached the life of adequate cognition. The highest good is therefore knowledge of God, and to know God is to enjoy the most nearly perfect happiness; while to entertain inadequate ideas is to give oneself over to the passions. The pleasure of blessedness so far exceeds the pleasure offered by the passions, that the truly self-seeking person will strive toward the understanding of God and cling to it. Only the emotion born of intuition and reason can conquer the petty appetites of daily life and keep those few who attain it, free and wise and secure.

Spinoza, the moralist, attacks the problems of human conduct with the same weapon he uses in theological matters, namely, pure reason. Experience teaches, he maintains, that man is subject to three basic passions: the passion for gold, the passion for honor, and the sex passion. As long as man is beset by any of these three, he is not his own master, but resembles rather a rudderless ship floundering in a sea of greeds. It is interesting to note that Spinoza does not speak of the libidinous nature of man as "immoral." By his standard, there is nothing in nature good or bad, evil or virtuous of itself. Things become good or bad only in relation to a third value. This value is Spinoza's concept of the quietude of the soul. Since he considers this quietude the greatest blessing and *summum bonum* of being, whatever keeps man from attaining it is negative, or bad, while whatever helps him reach this state of supreme happiness is positive, or good. Since reason is the only means by which man can master his raging passions, Spinoza considers their conquest an intellectual process.

To him, then, the wise man is *eo ipso* the free man, who no longer is pulled in every direction by greed, lust or ambition, but who, rather, in full consciousness of his inner self and his unity with the All, leads a life of spiritual independence and serenity. To reach such a rarefied state is, admittedly, an arduous task, possible to only a few select minds. But then, Spinoza reminds us, all things of grandeur are as rare as they are difficult.

D.D.R.

HOW TO IMPROVE
YOUR MIND

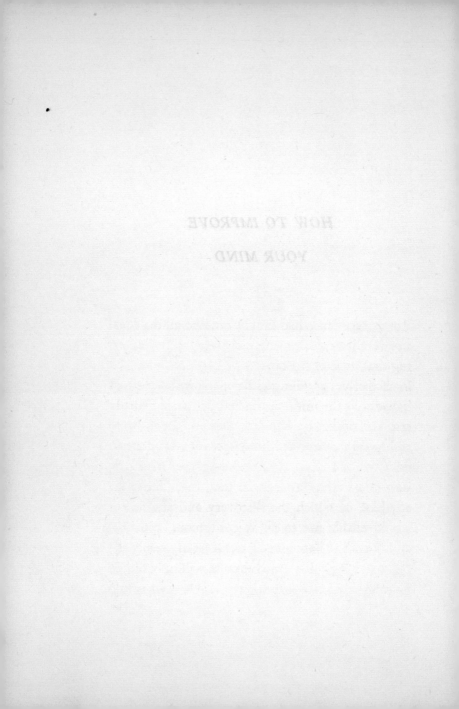

HOW TO IMPROVE

YOUR MIND

AFTER experience had taught me that all the usual surroundings of social life are vain and futile; seeing that none of the objects of my fears contained in themselves anything either good or bad, except in so far as the mind is affected by them, I finally resolved to inquire whether there might be some real good having power to communicate itself, which would affect the mind singly, to the exclusion of all else: whether, in fact, there might be anything of which the discovery and attainment would enable me to enjoy continuous, supreme, and unending happiness. I say "I *finally* resolved," for at first sight it seemed unwise willingly to lose hold on what was sure for the sake of something then uncertain. I could see the benefits which are acquired through fame and riches, and that I should be obliged to abandon the quest of such objects, if I seriously devoted myself to the search for something different and new. I perceived that if true happiness chanced to be placed in the former I should necessarily miss it; while if, on the other hand, it were not so placed, and I gave them my whole attention, I should equally fail.

I therefore debated whether it would not be possible to arrive at the new principle, or at any rate at a certainty concerning its existence, without changing the conduct and usual plan of my life; with this end in view I made many efforts, but in vain. For the ordinary surroundings of life which are esteemed by men (as their actions testify) to be the highest good, may be classed under the three heads—Riches, Fame, and the Pleasures of Sense: with these three the mind is so absorbed that it has little power to reflect on any different good. By sensual pleasure the mind is enthralled to the extent of quiescence, as if the supreme good were actually attained, so that it is quite incapable of thinking of any other object; when such pleasure has been gratified it is followed by extreme melancholy, whereby the mind, though not enthralled, is disturbed and dulled.

The pursuit of honours and riches is likewise very absorbing, especially if such objects be sought simply for their own sake,[1] inasmuch as they are then supposed to constitute the highest good. In the case of fame the mind is still more absorbed, for fame is conceived as always good for its own sake, and as the ultimate end to which all actions are directed. Further, the attainment of riches and fame is not followed as in the case of sensual pleasures by repentance, but, the more we acquire, the greater is our delight, and, consequently, the more are we incited to increase both the one and the other; on the other hand, if our hopes happen to be frustrated we are plunged into the deepest sadness. Fame has the further drawback that it

[1] *The pursuit of honours and riches is likewise very absorbing, especially if such objects be sought simply for their own sake.* This might be explained more at large and more clearly: I mean, by distinguishing riches according as they are pursued for their own sake, or in furtherance of fame, or sensual pleasure, or the advancement of science and art. But this subject is reserved to its own place, for it is not here proper to investigate the matter more accurately.

compels its votaries to order their lives according to the opinions of their fellow-men, shunning what they usually shun, and seeking what they usually seek.

When I saw that all these ordinary objects of desire would be obstacles in the way of a search for something different and new—nay, that they were so opposed thereto, that either they or it would have to be abandoned, I was forced to inquire which would prove the most useful to me: for, as I say, I seemed to be willingly losing hold on a sure good for the sake of something uncertain. However, after I had reflected on the matter, I came in the first place to the conclusion that by abandoning the ordinary objects of pursuit, and betaking myself to a new quest, I should be leaving a good, uncertain by reason of its own nature, as may be gathered from what has been said, for the sake of a good not uncertain in its nature (for I sought for a fixed good), but only in the possibility of its attainment.

Further reflection convinced me, that if I could really get to the root of the matter I should be leaving certain evils for a certain good. I thus perceived that I was in a state of great peril, and I compelled myself to seek with all my strength for a remedy, however uncertain it might be; as a sick man struggling with a deadly disease, when he sees that death will surely be upon him unless a remedy be found, is compelled to seek such a remedy with all his strength, inasmuch as his whole hope lies therein. All the objects pursued by the multitude not only bring no remedy that tends to preserve our being, but even act as hindrances, causing the death not seldom of those who possess them, and always of those who are possessed by them.[2] There are many examples of men who have suffered persecution even to death for the sake of their riches, and of men who in pursuit of wealth have exposed themselves to so many dangers, that they have paid away their life as a penalty for their folly. Examples are no less numerous of men, who have endured the utmost wretchedness for the sake of gaining or preserving their reputation. Lastly, there are innumerable cases of men, who have hastened their death through over-indulgence in sensual pleasure. All these evils seem to have arisen from the fact, that

[2] These considerations should be set forth more precisely.

happiness or unhappiness is made wholly to depend on the quality of the object which we love. When a thing is not loved, no quarrels will arise concerning it—no sadness will be felt if it perishes—no envy if it is possessed by another—no fear, no hatred, in short no disturbances of the mind. All these arise from the love of what is perishable, such as the objects already mentioned. But love towards a thing eternal and infinite feeds the mind wholly with joy, and is itself unmingled with any sadness, wherefore it is greatly to be desired and sought for with all our strength. Yet it was not at random that I used the words, "If I could go to the root of the matter," for, though what I have urged was perfectly clear to my mind, I could not forthwith lay aside all love of riches, sensual enjoyment, and fame. One thing was evident, namely, that while my mind was employed with these thoughts it turned away from its former objects of desire, and seriously considered the search for a new principle; this state of things was a great comfort to me, for I perceived that the evils were not such as to resist all remedies. Although these intervals were at first rare, and of very short duration, yet afterwards,

as the true good became more and more discerni-
ble to me, they became more frequent and more
lasting; especially after I had recognized that the
acquisition of wealth, sensual pleasure, or fame,
is only a hindrance, so long as they are sought as
ends not as means; if they be sought as means,
they will be under restraint, and, far from being
hindrances, will further not a little the end for
which they are sought, as I will show in due time.

I will here only briefly state what I mean by
true good, and also what is the nature of the
highest good. In order that this may be rightly
understood, we must bear in mind that the terms
good and evil are only applied relatively, so that
the same thing may be called both good and bad,
according to the relations in view, in the same
way as it may be called perfect or imperfect.
Nothing regarded in its own nature can be called
perfect or imperfect; especially when we are
aware that all things which come to pass, come to
pass according to the eternal order and fixed laws
of nature. However, human weakness cannot attain to this order in its own thoughts, but meanwhile man conceives a human character much
more stable than his own, and sees that there is

no reason why he should not himself acquire such a character. Thus he is led to seek for means which will bring him to this pitch of perfection, and calls everything which will serve as such means a true good. The chief good is that he should arrive, together with other individuals if possible, at the possession of the aforesaid character. What that character is we shall show in due time, namely, that it is the knowledge of the union existing between the mind and the whole of nature.[3] This, then, is the end for which I strive, to attain to such a character myself, and to endeavour that many should attain to it with me. In other words, it is part of my happiness to lend a helping hand, that many others may understand even as I do, so that their understanding and desire may entirely agree with my own. In order to bring this about, it is necessary to understand as much of nature as will enable us to attain to the aforesaid character, and also to form a social order such as is most conducive to the attainment of this character by the greatest number with the least difficulty and danger. We must

[3] These matters are explained more at length elsewhere.

seek the assistance of Moral Philosophy[4] and the Theory of Education; further, as health is no insignificant means for attaining our end, we must also include the whole science of Medicine, and, as many difficult things are by contrivance rendered easy, and we can in this way gain much time and convenience, the science of Mechanics must in no way be despised. But, before all things, a means must be devised for improving the understanding and purifying it, as far as may be at the outset, so that it may apprehend things without error, and in the best possible way.

Thus it is apparent to everyone that I wish to direct all sciences to one end and aim,[5] so that we may attain to the supreme human perfection which we have named; and, therefore, whatsoever in the sciences does not serve to promote our object will have to be rejected as useless. To sum up the matter in a word, all our actions and thoughts must be directed to this one end. Yet,

[4] N.B. I do no more here than enumerate the sciences necessary for our purpose; I lay no stress on their order.

[5] There is for the sciences but one end, to which they should all be directed.

as it is necessary that while we are endeavouring to attain our purpose, and bring the understanding into the right path, we should carry on our life, we are compelled first of all to lay down certain rules of life as provisionally good, to wit the following:—

I. To speak in a manner intelligible to the multitude, and to comply with every general custom that does not hinder the attainment of our purpose. For we can gain from the multitude no small advantages, provided that we strive to accommodate ourselves to its understanding as far as possible: moreover, we shall in this way gain a friendly audience for the reception of the truth.

II. To indulge ourselves with pleasures only in so far as they are necessary for preserving health.

III. Lastly, to endeavour to obtain only sufficient money or other commodities to enable us to preserve our life and health, and to follow such general customs as are consistent with our purpose.

Having laid down these preliminary rules, I will betake myself to the first and most important task, namely, the amendment of the understanding, and the rendering it capable of understanding things in the manner necessary for attaining our end.

In order to bring this about, the natural order demands that I should here recapitulate all the modes of perception, which I have hitherto employed for affirming or denying anything with certainty, so that I may choose the best, and at the same time begin to know my own powers and the nature which I wish to perfect.

Reflection shows that all modes of perception or knowledge may be reduced to four:—

I. Perception arising from hearsay or from some sign which everyone may name as he pleases.

II. Perception arising from mere experience— that is, from experience not yet classified by the intellect, and only so called because the given event has happened to take place, and we have no contradictory fact to set against it, so that it therefore remains unassailed in our mind.

III. Perception arising when the essence of one thing is inferred from another thing, but not adequately; this comes[6] when from some effect we

[6] In this case we do not understand anything of the cause from the consideration of it in the effect. This is

gather its cause, or when it is inferred from some general proposition that some property is always present.

IV. Lastly, there is the perception arising when a thing is perceived solely through its essence, or through the knowledge of its proximate cause.

All these kinds of perception I will illustrate by examples. By hearsay I know the day of my birth, my parentage, and other matters about which I have never felt any doubt. By mere experience I know that I shall die, for this I can affirm from having seen that others like myself have died, though all did not live for the same period, or die by the same disease. I know by mere experience that oil has the property of feeding fire, and water of extinguishing it. In the same way I know that a dog is a barking animal,

---

sufficiently evident from the fact that the cause is only spoken of in very general terms, such as—there exists then something; there exists then some power, &c.; or from the fact that we only express it in a negative manner—it is not this or that, &c. In the second case something is ascribed to the cause because of the effect, as we shall show in an example, but only a property, never the essence.

man a rational animal, and in fact nearly all the practical knowledge of life.

We deduce one thing from another as follows: when we clearly perceive that we feel a certain body and no other, we thence clearly infer that the mind is united to the body,[7] and that their union is the cause of the given sensation; but we cannot thence absolutely understand the nature of the sensation and the union.[8] Or, after I have be-

[7] From this example may be clearly seen what I have just drawn attention to. For through this union we understand nothing beyond the sensation, the effect, to wit, from which we inferred the cause of which we understand nothing.

[8] A conclusion of this sort, though it be certain, is yet not to be relied on without great caution; for unless we are exceedingly careful we shall forthwith fall into error. When things are conceived thus abstractedly, and not through their true essence, they are apt to be confused by the imagination. For that which is in itself one, men imagine to be multiplex. To those things which are conceived abstractedly, apart, and confusedly, terms are applied which are apt to become wrested from their strict meaning, and bestowed on things more familiar; whence it results that these latter are imagined in the same way as the former to which the terms were originally given.

come acquainted with the nature of vision, and know that it has the property of making one and the same thing appear smaller when far off than when near, I can infer that the sun is larger than it appears, and can draw other conclusions of the same kind.

Lastly, a thing may be perceived solely through its essence; when, from the fact of knowing something, I know what it is to know that thing, or when, from knowing the essence of the mind, I know that it is united to the body. By the same kind of knowledge we know that two and three make five, or that two lines each parallel to a third, are parallel to one another, &c. The things which I have been able to know by this kind of knowledge are as yet very few.

In order that the whole matter may be put in a clearer light, I will make use of a single illustration as follows. Three numbers are given—it is required to find a fourth, which shall be to the third as the second is to the first. Tradesmen will at once tell us that they know what is required to find the fourth number, for they have not yet forgotten the rule which was given to them arbitrarily without proof by their masters; others construct a universal axiom from their experience with simple numbers, where the fourth number is self-evident, as in the case of 2, 4, 3, 6; here it is evident that if the second number be multiplied by the third, and the product divided by the first, the quotient is 6; when they see that by this process the number is produced which they knew beforehand to be the proportional, they infer that the process always holds good for finding a fourth number proportional. Mathematicians, however, know by the proof of the nineteenth proposition of the seventh book of Euclid, what numbers are proportionals, namely, from the nature and property of proportion it follows that the product of the first and fourth will be equal to the product of the second and third: still they do not see the adequate proportionality of the given numbers, or, if they do see it, they see it not by virtue of Euclid's proposition, but intuitively, without going through any process.

In order that from these modes of perception the best may be selected, it is well that we should briefly enumerate the means necessary for attaining our end.

I. To have an exact knowledge of our nature

which we desire to perfect, and to know as much as is needful of nature in general.

II. To collect in this way the differences, the agreements, and the oppositions of things.

III. To learn thus exactly how far they can or cannot be modified.

IV. To compare this result with the nature and power of man. We shall thus discern the highest degree of perfection to which man is capable of attaining. We shall then be in a position to see which mode of perception we ought to choose.

As to the first mode, it is evident that from hearsay our knowledge must always be uncertain, and, moreover, can give us no insight into the essence of a thing, as is manifest in our illustration; now one can only arrive at knowledge of a thing through knowledge of its essence, as will hereafter appear. We may, therefore, clearly conclude that the certainty arising from hearsay cannot be scientific in its character. For simple hearsay cannot affect anyone whose understanding does not, so to speak, meet it half way.

The second mode of perception[*] cannot be said

[*] I shall here treat a little more in detail of experience, and shall examine the method adopted by the Empirics, and by recent philosophers.

to give us the idea of the proportion of which we are in search. Moreover its results are very uncertain and indefinite, for we shall never discover anything in natural phenomena by its means, except accidental properties, which are never clearly understood, unless the essence of the things in question be known first. Wherefore this mode also must be rejected.

Of the third mode of perception we may say in a manner that it gives us the idea of the thing sought, and that it enables us to draw conclusions without risk of error; yet it is not by itself sufficient to put us in possession of the perfection we aim at.

The fourth mode alone apprehends the adequate essence of a thing without danger of error. This mode, therefore, must be the one which we chiefly employ. How, then, should we avail ourselves of it so as to gain the fourth kind of knowledge with the least delay concerning things previously unknown? I will proceed to explain.

Now that we know what kind of knowledge is necessary for us, we must indicate the way and the method whereby we may gain the said knowledge concerning the things needful to be known. In order to accomplish this, we must first take

care not to commit ourselves to a search, going
back to infinity—that is, in order to discover the
best method for finding out the truth, there is no
need of another method to discover such method;
nor of a third method for discovering the second,
and so on to infinity. By such proceedings, we
should never arrive at the knowledge of the
truth, or, indeed, at any knowledge at all. The
matter stands on the same footing as the making
of material tools, which might be argued about
in a similar way. For, in order to work iron, a
hammer is needed, and the hammer cannot be
forthcoming unless it has been made; but, in order to make it, there was need of another hammer and other tools, and so on to infinity. We
might thus vainly endeavour to prove that men
have no power of working iron. But as men at
first made use of the instruments supplied by nature to accomplish very easy pieces of workmanship, laboriously and imperfectly, and then, when
these were finished, wrought other things more
difficult with less labour and greater perfection;
and so gradually mounted from the simplest operations to the making of tools, and from the making of tools to the making of more complex tools,

and fresh feats of workmanship, till they arrived at making, with small expenditure of labour, the vast number of complicated mechanisms which they now possess. So, in like manner, the intellect, by its native strength,[10] makes for itself intellectual instruments, whereby it acquires strength for performing other intellectual operations,[11] and from these operations gets again fresh instruments, or the power of pushing its investigations further, and thus gradually proceeds till it reaches the summit of wisdom.

That this is the path pursued by the understanding may be readily seen, when we understand the nature of the method for finding out the truth, and of the natural instruments so necessary for the construction of more complex instruments, and for the progress of investigation. I thus proceed with my demonstration.

A true idea[12] (for we possess a true idea) is

[10] By native strength, I mean that bestowed on us by external causes, as I shall afterwards explain in my philosophy.

[11] I here term them operations: I shall explain their nature in my philosophy.

[12] I shall take care not only to demonstrate what I have just advanced, but also that we have hitherto proceeded rightly, and other things needful to be known.

something different from its correlate (*ideatum*);
thus a circle is different from the idea of a circle.
The idea of a circle is not something having a
circumference and a centre, as a circle has; nor is
the idea of a body that body itself. Now, as it is
something different from its correlate, it is capable of being understood through itself; in other
words, the idea, in so far as its actual essence
(*essentia formalis*) is concerned, may be the subject of another subjective essence (*essentia objec-
tiva*).[13] And, again, this second subjective essence
will, regarded in itself, be something real, and
capable of being understood; and so on, indefinitely. For instance, the man Peter is something
real; the true idea of Peter is the reality of Peter
represented subjectively, and is in itself something
real, and quite distinct from the actual Peter.
Now, as this true idea of Peter is in itself something real, and has its own individual existence,
it will also be capable of being understood—that
is, of being the subject of another idea, which will

[13] In modern language, "the idea may become the subject of another representation." *Objectivus* generally cor-
responds to the modern "subjective," *formalis* to the
modern "objective."—[Tr.]

contain by representation (*objective*) all that the idea of Peter contains actually (*formaliter*). And, again, this idea of the idea of Peter has its own individuality, which may become the subject of yet another idea; and so on, indefinitely. This everyone may make trial of for himself, by reflecting that he knows what Peter is, and also knows that he knows, and further knows that he knows that he knows, &c. Hence it is plain that, in order to understand the actual Peter, it is not necessary first to understand the idea of Peter, and still less the idea of the idea of Peter. This is the same as saying that, in order to know, there is no need to know that we know, much less to know that we know that we know. This is no more necessary than to know the nature of a circle before knowing the nature of a triangle.[14] But, with these ideas, the contrary is the case: for, in order to know that I know, I must first know. Hence it is clear that certainty is nothing else than the sub-

---

[14] Observe that we are not here inquiring how this first subjective essence is innate in us. This belongs to an investigation into nature, where all these matters are amply explained, and it is shown that without ideas neither affirmation, nor negation, nor volition are possible.

jective essence of a thing: in other words, the mode in which we perceive an actual reality is certainty. Further, it is also evident that, for the certitude of truth, no further sign is necessary beyond the possession of a true idea: for, as I have shown, it is not necessary to know that we know that we know. Hence, again, it is clear that no one can know the nature of the highest certainty, unless he possesses an adequate idea, or the subjective essence of a thing: for certainty is identical with such subjective essence. Thus, as the truth needs no sign—it being sufficient to possess the subjective essence of things, or, in other words, the ideas of them, in order that all doubts may be removed —it follows that the true method does not consist in seeking for the signs of truth after the acquisition of the idea, but that the true method teaches us the order in which we should seek for truth itself,[15] or the subjective essences of things, or ideas, for all these expressions are synonymous. Again, method must necessarily be concerned with reasoning or understanding—I mean, method is not identical with reasoning in the

[15] The nature of mental search is explained in my philosophy.

search for causes, still less is it the comprehension of the causes of things: it is the discernment of a true idea, by distinguishing it from other perceptions, and by investigating its nature, in order that we may thus know our power of understanding, and may so train our mind that it may, by a given standard, comprehend whatsoever is intelligible, by laying down certain rules as aids, and by avoiding useless mental exertion.

Whence we may gather that method is nothing else than reflective knowledge, or the idea of an idea; and that as there can be no idea of an idea—unless an idea exists previously,—there can be no method without a pre-existent idea. Therefore, that will be a good method which shows us how the mind should be directed, according to the standard of the given true idea.

Again, seeing that the ratio existing between two ideas is the same as the ratio between the actual realities corresponding to those ideas, it follows that the reflective knowledge which has for its object the most perfect being is more excellent than reflective knowledge concerning other objects—in other words, that method will be most perfect which affords the standard of the given idea of the most perfect being whereby we **may** direct our mind. We thus easily understand how, in proportion as it acquires new ideas, the mind simultaneously acquires fresh instruments for pursuing its inquiries further. For we may gather from what has been said, that a true idea must necessarily first of all exist in us as a natural instrument; and that when this idea is apprehended by the mind, it enables us to understand the difference existing between itself and all other perceptions. In this, one part of the method consists.

Now it is clear that the mind apprehends itself better in proportion as it understands a greater number of natural objects; it follows, therefore, that this portion of the method will be more perfect in proportion as the mind attains to the comprehension of a greater number of objects, and that it will be absolutely perfect when the mind gains a knowledge of the absolutely perfect being, or becomes conscious thereof. Again, the more things the mind knows, the better does it understand its own strength and the order of nature; by increased self-knowledge, it can direct itself more easily, and lay down rules for its own guidance;

and, by increased knowledge of nature, it can more easily avoid what is useless.

And this is the sum total of method, as we have already stated. We may add that the idea in the world of thought is in the same case as its correlate in the world of reality. If, therefore, there be anything in nature which is without connection[16] with any other thing, and if we assign to it a subjective essence, which would in every way correspond to the objective reality, the subjective essence would have no connection with any other ideas—in other words, we could not draw any conclusion with regard to it. On the other hand, those things which are connected with others—as all things that exist in nature—will be understood by the mind, and their subjective essences will maintain the same mutual relations as their objective realities—that is to say, we shall infer from these ideas other ideas, which will in turn be connected with others, and thus our instruments for proceeding with our investigation will increase. This is what we were endeavouring to

[16] To be connected with other things is to be produced by them, or to produce them.

41

prove. Further, from what has just been said—namely, that an idea must, in all respects, correspond to its correlate in the world of reality,—it is evident that, in order to reproduce in every respect the faithful image of nature, our mind must deduce all its ideas from the idea which represents the origin and source of the whole of nature, so that it may itself become the source of other ideas.

It may, perhaps, provoke astonishment that, after having said that the good method is that which teaches us to direct our mind according to the standard of the given true idea, we should prove our point by reasoning, which would seem to indicate that it is not self-evident. We may, therefore, be questioned as to the validity of our reasoning. If our reasoning be sound, we must take as a starting-point a true idea. Now, to be certain that our starting-point is really a true idea, we need a proof. This first course of reasoning must be supported by a second, the second by a third, and so on to infinity. To this I make answer that, if by some happy chance anyone had adopted this method in his investigations of nature—that is, if he had acquired new ideas in the proper order, according to the standard of the original true idea, he would never have doubted of the truth of his knowledge,[17] inasmuch as truth, as we have shown, makes itself manifest, and all things would flow, as it were, spontaneously towards him. But as this never, or rarely, happens, I have been forced so to arrange my proceedings, that we may acquire by reflection and forethought what we cannot acquire by chance, and that it may at the same time appear that, for proving the truth, and for valid reasoning, we need no other means than the truth and valid reasoning themselves: for by valid reasoning I have established valid reasoning, and, in like measure, I seek still to establish it. Moreover, this is the order of thinking adopted by men in their inward meditations. The reasons for its rare employment in investigations of nature are to be found in current misconceptions, whereof we shall examine the causes hereafter in our philosophy. Moreover, it demands, as we shall show, a keen and accurate discernment. Lastly, it is hindered by the conditions of human life, which are, as we have already pointed out, extremely change-

[17] In the same way as we have here no doubt of the truth of our knowledge.

able. There are also other obstacles, which we will not here inquire into.

If anyone asks why I have not at the starting-point set forth all the truths of nature in their due order, inasmuch as truth is self-evident, I reply by warning him not to reject as false any paradoxes he may find here, but to take the trouble to reflect on the chain of reasoning by which they are supported; he will then be no longer in doubt that we have attained to the truth. This is why I have begun as above.

If there yet remains some sceptic, who doubts of our primary truth, and of all deductions we make, taking such truth as our standard, he must either be arguing in bad faith, or we must confess that there are men in complete mental blindness, either innate or due to misconceptions—that is, to some external influence.

Such persons are not conscious of themselves. If they affirm or doubt anything, they know not that they affirm or doubt: they say that they know nothing, and they say that they are ignorant of the very fact of their knowing nothing. Even this they do not affirm absolutely, they are afraid of confessing that they exist, so long as they know nothing; in fact, they ought to remain dumb, for fear of haply supposing something which should smack of truth. Lastly, with such persons, one should not speak of sciences: for, in what relates to life and conduct, they are compelled by necessity to suppose that they exist, and seek their own advantage, and often affirm and deny, even with an oath. If they deny, grant, or gainsay, they know not that they deny, grant, or gainsay, so that they ought to be regarded as automata, utterly devoid of intelligence.

Let us now return to our proposition. Up to the present, we have, first, defined the end to which we desire to direct all our thoughts; secondly, we have determined the mode of perception best adapted to aid us in attaining our perfection; thirdly, we have discovered the way which our mind should take, in order to make a good beginning—namely, that it should use every true idea as a standard in pursuing its inquiries according to fixed rules. Now, in order that it may thus proceed, our method must furnish us, first, with a means of distinguishing a true idea from all other perceptions, and enabling the mind to avoid the latter; secondly, with rules for perceiving unknown things according to the standard of the true idea; thirdly, with an order which enables us to avoid useless labour. When we became acquainted with this method, we saw that, fourthly, it would be perfect when we had attained to the idea of the absolutely perfect Being. This is an observation which should be made at the outset, in order that we may arrive at the knowledge of such a being more quickly.

Let us then make a beginning with the first part of the method, which is, as we have said, to distinguish and separate the true idea from other perceptions, and to keep the mind from confusing with true ideas those which are false, fictitious, and doubtful. I intend to dwell on this point at length, partly to keep a distinction so necessary before the reader's mind, and also because there are some who doubt of true ideas, through not having attended to the distinction between a true perception and all others. Such persons are like men who, while they are awake, doubt not that they are awake, but afterwards in a dream, as often happens, thinking that they are surely awake, and then finding that they were in error, become doubtful even of being awake. This state of mind arises through neglect of the distinction between sleeping and waking.

Meanwhile, I give warning that I shall not here give the essence of every perception, and explain it through its proximate cause. Such work lies in the province of philosophy. I shall confine myself to what concerns method—that is, to the character of fictitious, false, and doubtful perception, and the means of freeing ourselves therefrom. Let us then first inquire into the nature of a fictitious idea.

Every perception has for its object either a thing considered as existing, or solely the essence of a thing. Now "fiction" is chiefly occupied with things considered as existing. I will, therefore, consider these first—I mean cases where only the existence of an object is feigned, and the thing thus feigned is understood, or assumed to be understood. For instance, I feign that Peter, whom I know to have gone home, is gone to see me,[18] or something of that kind. With what is such an idea concerned? It is concerned with things possi-

[18] See below the note on hypotheses, whereof we have a clear understanding; the fiction consists in saying that such hypotheses exist in heavenly bodies.

ble, and not with things necessary or impossible. I call a thing *impossible* when its existence would imply a contradiction; *necessary,* when its non-existence would imply a contradiction; *possible,* when neither its existence nor its non-existence implies a contradiction, but when the necessity or impossibility of its nature depends on causes unknown to us, while we feign that it exists. If the necessity or impossibility of its existence depending on external causes were known to us, we could not form any fictitious hypothesis about it; whence it follows that if there be a God, or omniscient Being, such an one cannot form fictitious hypotheses. For, as regards ourselves, when I know that I exist, I cannot hypothesize that I exist or do not exist[19] any more than I can hypothesize an elephant that can go through the eye of a needle; nor when I know the nature of God, can I hypothesize that He exists or does not

[19] As a thing, when once it is understood, manifests itself, we have need only of an example without further proof. In the same way the contrary has only to be presented to our minds to be recognized as false, as will forthwith appear when we come to discuss fiction concerning essences.

exist.[20] The same thing must be said of the Chimæra, whereof the nature implies a contradiction. From these considerations, it is plain, as I have already stated, that fiction cannot be concerned with eternal truths.[21]

But before proceeding further, I must remark, in passing, that the difference between the essence of one thing and the essence of another thing is the same as that which exists between the reality or existence of one thing and the reality or existence of another; therefore, if we wished to conceive the existence, for example, of Adam, simply by means of existence in general, it would be the same as if, in order to conceive his existence, we

[20] Observe, that although many assert that they doubt whether God exists, they have nought but his name in their minds, or else some fiction which they call God: this fiction is not in harmony with God's real nature, as we will duly show.

[21] I shall presently show that no fiction can concern eternal truths. By an eternal truth, I mean that which being positive could never become negative. Thus it is a primary and eternal truth that *God exists,* but it is not an eternal truth that *Adam thinks.* That the *Chimæra does not exist* is an eternal truth, that *Adam does not think* is not so.

went back to the nature of being, so as to define Adam as a being. Thus, the more existence is conceived generally, the more is it conceived confusedly, and the more easily can it be ascribed to a given object. Contrariwise, the more it is conceived particularly, the more is it understood clearly, and the less liable is it to be ascribed, through negligence of Nature's order, to anything save its proper object. This is worthy of remark.

We now proceed to consider those cases which are commonly called fictions, though we clearly understand that the thing is not as we imagine it. For instance, I know that the earth is round, but nothing prevents my telling people that it is a hemisphere, and that it is like a half apple carved in relief on a dish; or, that the sun moves round the earth, and so on. However, examination will show us that there is nothing here inconsistent with what has been said, provided we first admit that we may have made mistakes, and be now conscious of them; and, further, that we can hypothesize, or at least suppose, that others are under the same mistake as ourselves, or can, like us, fall under it. We can, I repeat, thus hypothesize so long as we see no impossibility. Thus, when I tell anyone that the earth is not round, &c., I merely recall the error which I perhaps made myself, or which I might have fallen into, and afterwards I hypothesize that the person to whom I tell it, is still, or may still fall under the same mistake. This I say, I can feign so long as I do not perceive any impossibility or necessity; if I truly understood either one or the other I should not be able to feign, and I should be reduced to saying that I had made the attempt.

It remains for us to consider hypotheses made in problems, which sometimes involve impossibilities. For instance, when we say—let us assume that this burning candle is not burning, or, let us assume that it burns in some imaginary space, or where there are no physical objects. Such assumptions are freely made, though the last is clearly seen to be impossible. But, though this be so, there is no fiction in the case. For, in the first case, I have merely recalled to memory another candle[22] not burning, or conceived the candle be-

[22] Afterwards, when we come to speak of fiction that is concerned with essences, it will be evident that fiction never creates or furnishes the mind with anything new;

fore me as without a flame, and then I understand
as applying to the latter, leaving its flame out of
the question, all that I think of the former. In the
second case, I have merely to abstract my thoughts
from the objects surrounding the candle, for the
mind to devote itself to the contemplation of the
candle singly looked at in itself only; I can then
draw the conclusion that the candle contains in
itself no cause for its own destruction, so that if
there were no physical objects the candle, and
even the flame, would remain unchangeable, and
so on. Thus there is here no fiction, but true
and bare assertions.[23]

only such things as are already in the brain or imagination are recalled to the memory, when the attention is
directed to them confusedly and all at once. For instance,
we have remembrance of spoken words and of a tree;
when the mind directs itself to them confusedly, it forms
the notion of a tree speaking. The same may be said of
existence, especially when it is conceived quite generally
as entity; it is then readily applied to all things occurring
together in the memory. This is specially worthy of remark.

[23] We must understand as much in the case of hypotheses put forward to explain certain movements ac-
companying celestial phenomena; but from these, when
applied to the celestial motions, we may draw conclusions

Let us now pass on to the fictions concerned with essences only, or with some reality or existence simultaneously. Of these we must specially observe that in proportion as the mind's understanding is smaller, and its experience multiplex, so will its power of coining fictions be larger, whereas as its understanding increases, its capacity for entertaining fictitious ideas becomes less. For instance, in the same way as we are unable, while we are thinking, to feign that we are thinking or not thinking, so, also, when we know the nature of body we cannot imagine an infinite fly; or, when we know the nature of the soul,[24] we cannot imagine it as square, though anything may be expressed verbally. But, as we said above, the less

as to the nature of the heavens, whereas this last may be quite different, especially as many other causes are conceivable which would account for such motions.

[24] It often happens that a man recalls to mind this word soul, and forms at the same time some corporeal image: as the two representations are simultaneous, he easily thinks that he imagines and feigns a corporeal soul: thus confusing the name with the thing itself. I here beg that my readers will not be in a hurry to refute this proposition; they will, I hope, have no mind to do so, if they pay close attention to the examples given and to what follows.

53

men know of nature the more easily can they coin fictitious ideas, such as trees speaking, men instantly changed into stones, or into fountains, ghosts appearing in mirrors, something issuing from nothing, even gods changed into beasts and men, and infinite other absurdities of the same kind.

Some persons think, perhaps, that fiction is limited by fiction, and not by understanding; in other words, after I have formed some fictitious idea, and have affirmed of my own free will that it exists under a certain form in nature, I am thereby precluded from thinking of it under any other form. For instance, when I have feigned (to repeat their argument) that the nature of body is of a certain kind, and have of my own free will desired to convince myself that it actually exists under this form, I am no longer able to hypothesize that a fly, for example, is infinite; so, when I have hypothesized the essence of the soul, I am not able to think of it as square, &c. But these arguments demand further inquiry. First, their upholders must either grant or deny that we can understand anything. If they grant it, then necessarily the same must be said of understanding, as is said of fiction. If they deny it, let us, who know that we do know something, see what they mean. They assert that the soul can be conscious of, and perceive in a variety of ways, not itself nor things which exist, but only things which are neither in itself nor anywhere else, in other words, that the soul can, by its unaided power, create sensations or ideas unconnected with things. In fact, they regard the soul as a sort of god. Further, they assert that we or our soul have such freedom that we can constrain ourselves, or our soul, or even our soul's freedom. For, after it has formed a fictitious idea, and has given its assent thereto, it cannot think or feign it in any other manner, but is constrained by the first fictitious idea to keep all its other thoughts in harmony therewith. Our opponents are thus driven to admit, in support of their fiction, the absurdities which I have just enumerated; and which are not worthy of rational refutation.[25]

[25] Though I seem to deduce this from experience, some may deny its cogency because I have given no formal proof. I therefore append the following for those who may desire it. As there can be nothing in nature contrary to nature's laws, since all things come to pass by fixed

While leaving such persons in their error, we will take care to derive from our argument with them a truth serviceable for our purpose, namely, that the mind, in paying attention to a thing hypothetical or false, so as to meditate upon it and understand it, and derive the proper conclusions in due order therefrom, will readily discover its falsity; and if the thing hypothetical be in its nature true, and the mind pays attention to it, so as to understand it, and deduce the truths which are derivable from it, the mind will proceed with an uninterrupted series of apt conclusions; in the same way as it would at once discover (as we showed just now) the absurdity of a false hypothesis, and of the conclusions drawn from it.

We need, therefore, be in no fear of forming hypotheses, so long as we have a clear and distinct perception of what is involved. For, if we were to assert, haply, that men are suddenly turned into beasts, the statement would be extremely general,

------

laws, so that each thing must irrefragably produce its own proper effect, it follows that the soul, as soon as it possesses the true conception of a thing, proceeds to reproduce in thought that thing's effects. See below, where I speak of the false idea.

so general that there would be no conception, that is, no idea or connection of subject and predicate, in our mind. If there were such a conception we should at the same time be aware of the means and the causes whereby the event took place. Moreover, we pay no attention to the nature of the subject and the predicate. Now, if the first idea be not fictitious, and if all the other ideas be deduced therefrom, our hurry to form fictitious ideas will gradually subside. Further, as a fictitious idea cannot be clear and distinct, but is necessarily confused, and as all confusion arises from the fact that the mind has only partial knowledge of a thing either simple or complex, and does not distinguish between the known and the unknown, and, again, that it directs its attention promiscuously to all parts of an object at once without making distinctions, it follows, *first,* that if the idea be of something very simple, it must necessarily be clear and distinct. For a very simple object cannot be known in part, it must either be known altogether or not at all. *Secondly,* it follows that if a complex object be divided by thought into a number of simple component parts, and if each part be regarded separately, all

confusion will disappear. *Thirdly,* it follows that
fiction cannot be simple, but is made up of the
blending of several confused ideas of diverse objects or actions existent in nature, or rather is composed of attention[26] directed to all such ideas at
once, and unaccompanied by any mental assent.

Now a fiction that was simple would be clear
and distinct, and therefore true, also a fiction
composed only of distinct ideas would be clear
and distinct, and therefore true. For instance,
when we know the nature of the circle and the
square, it is impossible for us to blend together
these two figures, and to hypothesize a square
circle, any more than a square soul, or things of
that kind. Let us shortly come to our conclusion,
and again repeat that we need have no fear of
confusing with true ideas that which is only a
fiction. As for the first sort of fiction of which we

[26] Observe that fiction regarded in itself, only differs
from dreams in that in the latter we do not perceive the
external causes which we perceive through the senses
while awake. It has hence been inferred that representations occurring in sleep have no connection with objects
external to us. We shall presently see that error is the
dreaming of a waking man: if it reaches a certain pitch
it becomes delirium.

have already spoken, when a thing is clearly conceived, we saw that if the existence of that thing is in itself an eternal truth, fiction can have no part in it; but if the existence of the thing conceived be not an eternal truth, we have only to be careful that such existence be compared to the thing's essence, and to consider the order of nature. As for the second sort of fiction, which we stated to be the result of simultaneously directing the attention, without the assent of the intellect, to different confused ideas representing different things and actions existing in nature, we have seen that an absolutely simple thing cannot be feigned, but must be understood, and that a complex thing is in the same case if we regard separately the simple parts whereof it is composed; we shall not even be able to hypothesize any untrue action concerning such objects, for we shall be obliged to consider at the same time the causes and the manner of such action.

These matters being thus understood, let us pass on to consider the false idea, observing the objects with which it is concerned, and the means of guarding ourselves from falling into false perceptions. Neither of these tasks will present much difficulty, after our inquiry concerning fictitious ideas. The false idea only differs from the fictitious idea in the fact of implying a mental assent—that is, as we have already remarked, while the representations are occurring, there are no causes present to us, wherefrom, as in fiction, we can conclude that such representations do not arise from external objects: in fact, it is much the same as dreaming with our eyes open, or while awake. Thus, a false idea is concerned with, or (to speak more correctly) attributable to, the existence of a thing whereof the essence is known, or the essence itself, in the same way as a fictitious idea. If attributable to the existence of the thing, it is corrected in the same way as a fictitious idea under similar circumstances. If attributable to the essence, it is likewise corrected in the same way as a fictitious idea. For if the nature of the thing known implies necessary existence, we cannot possibly be in error with regard to its existence; but if the nature of the thing be not an eternal truth, like its essence, but contrariwise the necessity or impossibility of its existence depends on external causes, then we must follow the same course as we adopted in the case of fiction, for it is corrected in the same manner. As for false ideas concerned with essences, or even with actions, such perceptions are necessarily always confused, being compounded of different confused perceptions of things existing in nature, as, for instance, when men are persuaded that deities are present in woods, in statues, in brute beasts, and the like; that there are bodies which, by their composition alone, give rise to intellect; that corpses reason, walk about, and speak; that God is deceived, and so on. But ideas which are clear and distinct can never be false: for ideas of things clearly and distinctly conceived are either very simple themselves, or are compounded from very simple ideas —that is, are deduced therefrom. The impossibility of a very simple idea being false is evident to everyone who understands the nature of truth or understanding and of falsehood.

As regards that which constitutes the reality of truth, it is certain that a true idea is distinguished from a false one, not so much by its extrinsic object as by its intrinsic nature. If an architect conceives a building properly constructed, though such a building may never have existed, and may never exist, nevertheless the idea is true; and the idea remains the same, whether it be put into execution or not. On the other hand, if anyone asserts, for instance, that Peter exists, without knowing whether Peter really exists or not, the assertion, as far as its asserter is concerned, is false, or not true, even though Peter actually does exist. The assertion that Peter exists is true only with regard to him who knows for certain that Peter does exist. Whence it follows that there is in ideas something real, whereby the true are distinguished from the false. This reality must be inquired into, if we are to find the best standard of truth (we have said that we ought to determine our thoughts by the given standard of a true idea, and that method is reflective knowledge), and to know the properties of our understanding. Neither must we say that the difference between true and false arises from the fact, that true knowledge consists in knowing things through their primary causes, wherein it is totally different from false knowledge, as I have just explained it: for thought is said to be true, if it involves subjectively the essence of any principle which has no cause, and is known through itself and in itself. Wherefore the reality (*forma*) of true thought

must exist in the thought itself, without reference
to other thoughts; it does not acknowledge the
object as its cause, but must depend on the actual
power and nature of the understanding. For, if
we suppose that the understanding has perceived
some new entity which has never existed, as some
conceive the understanding of God before He
created things (a perception which certainly
could not arise from any object), and has legiti-
mately deduced other thoughts from the said perception, all such thoughts would be true, without
being determined by any external object; they
would depend solely on the power and nature of
the understanding. Thus, that which constitutes
the reality of a true thought must be sought in
the thought itself, and deduced from the nature
of the understanding. In order to pursue our investigation, let us confront ourselves with some
true idea, whose object we know for certain to be
dependent on our power of thinking, and to have
nothing corresponding to it in nature. With an
idea of this kind before us, we shall, as appears
from what has just been said, be more easily able
to carry on the research we have in view. For
instance, in order to form the conception of a

sphere, I invent a cause at my pleasure—namely, a semicircle revolving round its centre, and thus producing a sphere. This is indisputably a true idea; and, although we know that no sphere in nature has ever actually been so formed, the perception remains true, and is the easiest manner of conceiving a sphere. We must observe that this perception asserts the rotation of a semicircle—which assertion would be false, if it were not associated with the conception of a sphere, or of a cause determining a motion of the kind, or absolutely, if the assertion were isolated. The mind would then only tend to the affirmation of the sole motion of a semicircle, which is not contained in the conception of a semicircle, and does not arise from the conception of any cause capable of producing such motion.

Thus *falsity* consists only in this, that something is affirmed of a thing, which is not contained in the conception we have formed of that thing, as motion or rest of a semicircle. Whence it follows that simple ideas cannot be other than *true* —*e.g.* the simple idea of a semicircle, of motion, of rest, of quantity, &c.

Whatsoever affirmation such ideas contain is

equal to the concept formed, and does not ex
further. Wherefore we may form as many sin
ideas as we please, without any fear of erron
only remains for us to inquire by what power
mind can form true ideas, and how far su
power extends. It is certain that such power ca
not extend itself infinitely. For when we affir
somewhat of a thing, which is not contained in
the concept we have formed of that thing, such
an affirmation shows a defect of our perception,
or that we have formed fragmentary or mutilated
ideas. Thus we have seen that the motion of a
semicircle is false when it is isolated in the mind,
but true when it is associated with the concept of
a sphere, or of some cause determining such a motion. But if it be the nature of a thinking being,
as seems, *primâ facie,* to be the case, to form true
or adequate thoughts, it is plain that inadequate
ideas arise in us only because we are parts of a
thinking being, whose thoughts—some in their
entirety, others in fragments only—constitute our
mind.

But there is another point to be considered,
which was not worth raising in the case of fiction,
but which gives rise to complete deception—

namely, that certain things presented to the imagination also exist in the understanding—in other words, are conceived clearly and distinctly. Hence, so long as we do not separate that which is distinct from that which is confused, certainty, or the true idea, becomes mixed with indistinct ideas. For instance, certain Stoics heard, perhaps, the term "soul," and also that the soul is immortal, yet imagined it only confusedly; they imagined, also, and understood that very subtle bodies penetrate all others, and are penetrated by none. By combining these ideas, and being at the same time certain of the truth of the axiom, they forthwith became convinced that the mind consists of very subtle bodies; that these very subtle bodies cannot be divided, &c. But we are freed from mistakes of this kind, so long as we endeavour to examine all our perceptions by the standard of the given true idea. We must take care, as has been said, to separate such perceptions from all those which arise from hearsay or unclassified experience.

Moreover, such mistakes arise from things being conceived too much in the abstract; for it is sufficiently self-evident that what I conceive as in

its true object I cannot apply to anything else. Lastly, they arise from a want of understanding of the primary elements of nature as a whole; whence we proceed without due order, and confound nature with abstract rules, which, although they be true enough in their sphere, yet, when misapplied, confound themselves, and pervert the order of nature. However, if we proceed with as little abstraction as possible, and begin from primary elements—that is, from the source and origin of nature, as far back as we can reach,—we need not fear any deceptions of this kind. As far as the knowledge of the origin of nature is concerned, there is no danger of our confounding it with abstractions. For when a thing is conceived in the abstract, as are all universal notions, the said universal notions are always more extensive in the mind than the number of individuals forming their contents really existing in nature.

Again, there are many things in nature, the difference between which is so slight as to be hardly perceptible to the understanding; so that it may readily happen that such things are confounded together, if they be conceived abstractedly. But since the first principle of nature cannot (as we shall see hereafter) be conceived abstractedly or universally, and cannot extend further in the understanding than it does in reality, and has no likeness to mutable things, no confusion need be feared in respect to the idea of it, provided (as before shown) that we possess a standard of truth. This is, in fact, a being single[27] and infinite; in other words, it is the sum total of being,[28] beyond which there is no being found.

Thus far we have treated of the false idea. We have now to investigate the doubtful idea—that is, to inquire what can cause us to doubt, and how doubt may be removed. I speak of real doubt existing in the mind, not of such doubt as we see exemplified when a man says that he doubts, though his mind does not really hesitate. The cure of the latter does not fall within the province of method, it belongs rather to inquiries concerning obstinacy and its cure. Real doubt is never produced in the mind by the thing doubted of. In

[27] These are not attributes of God displaying His essence, as I will show in my philosophy.

[28] This has been shown already. For if such a being did not exist it would never be produced: therefore the mind would be able to understand more than nature could furnish; and this has been shown above to be false.

other words, if there were only one idea in the mind, whether that idea were true or false, there would be no doubt or certainty present, only a certain sensation. For an idea is in itself nothing else than a certain sensation; but doubt will arise through another idea, not clear and distinct enough for us to be able to draw any certain conclusion with regard to the matter under consideration; that is, the idea which causes us to doubt is not clear and distinct. To take an example. Supposing that a man has never reflected, taught by experience, or by any other means, that our senses sometimes deceive us, he will never doubt whether the sun be greater or less than it appears. Thus rustics are generally astonished when they hear that the sun is much larger than the earth. But from reflection on the deceitfulness of the senses[29] doubt arises, and if, after doubting, we acquire a true knowledge of the senses, and how things at a distance are represented through their instrumentality, doubt is again removed. Hence we cannot cast doubt on true ideas by the supposition

[29] That is, it is known that the senses sometimes deceive us. But it is only known confusedly, for it is not known how they deceive us.

that there is a deceitful Deity, who leads us astray even in what is most certain. We can only hold such an hypothesis so long as we have no clear and distinct idea—in other words, until we reflect on the knowledge which we have of the first principle of all things, and find that which teaches us that God is not a deceiver, and until we know this with the same certainty as we know from reflecting on the nature of a triangle that its three angles are equal to two right angles. But if we have a knowledge of God equal to that which we have of a triangle, all doubt is removed. In the same way as we can arrive at the said knowledge of a triangle, though not absolutely sure that there is not some arch-deceiver leading us astray, so can we come to a like knowledge of God under the like condition, and when we have attained to it, it is sufficient, as I said before, to remove every doubt which we can possess concerning clear and distinct ideas. Thus, if a man proceeded with our investigations in due order, inquiring first into those things which should first be inquired into, never passing over a link in the chain of association, and with knowledge how to define his questions before seeking to answer them, he will never have any ideas save such as are very certain, or, in other words, clear and distinct; for doubt is only a suspension of the spirit concerning some affirmation or negation which it would pronounce upon unhesitatingly if it were not in ignorance of something, without which the knowledge of the matter in hand must needs be imperfect. We may, therefore, conclude that doubt always proceeds from want of due order in investigation.

These are the points I promised to discuss in this first part of my treatise on method. However, in order not to omit anything which can conduce to the knowledge of the understanding and its faculties, I will add a few words on the subject of memory and forgetfulness.

The point most worthy of attention is, that memory is strengthened both with and without the aid of the understanding. For the more intelligible a thing is, the more easily is it remembered, and the less intelligible it is, the more easily do we forget it. For instance, a number of unconnected words is much more difficult to remember than the same number in the form of a narration. The memory is also strengthened without the aid of the understanding by means of the power wherewith the imagination or the sense called common is affected by some particular physical object. I say *particular,* for the imagination is only affected by particular objects. If we read, for instance, a single romantic comedy, we shall remember it very well, so long as we do not read many others of the same kind, for it will reign alone in the memory. If, however, we read several others of the same kind, we shall think of them altogether, and easily confuse one with another. I say, also, *physical.* For the imagination is only affected by physical objects. As, then, the memory is strengthened both with and without the aid of the understanding, we may conclude that it is different from the understanding, and that in the latter considered in itself there is neither memory nor forgetfulness. What, then, is memory? It is nothing else than the actual sensation of impressions on the brain, accompanied with the thought of a definite duration of the sensation.[30] This is also shown by reminiscence.

[30] If the duration be indefinite, the recollection is imperfect; this everyone seems to have learnt from nature. For we often ask, to strengthen our belief in something we hear of, when and where it happened; though ideas

For then we think of the sensation, but without the notion of continuous duration; thus the idea of that sensation is not the actual duration of the sensation or actual memory. Whether ideas are or are not subject to corruption will be seen in my philosophy. If this seems too absurd to anyone, it will be sufficient for our purpose, if he reflect on the fact that a thing is more easily remembered in proportion to its singularity, as appears from the example of the comedy just cited. Further, a thing is remembered more easily in proportion to its intelligibility; therefore we cannot help remembering that which is extremely singular and sufficiently intelligible.

Thus, then, we have distinguished between a true idea and other perceptions, and shown that ideas fictitious, false, and the rest, originate in the imagination—that is, in certain sensations fortuitous, so to speak and disconnected, arising not from the power of the mind, but from external

---

themselves have their own duration in the mind, yet, as we are wont to determine duration by the aid of some measure of motion which, again, takes place by aid of the imagination, we preserve no memory connected with pure intellect.

causes, according as the body, sleeping or waking, receives various motions.

But one may take any view one likes of the imagination so long as one acknowledges that it is different from the understanding, and that the soul is passive with regard to it. The view taken is immaterial, if we know that the imagination is something indefinite, with regard to which the soul is passive, and that we can by some means or other free ourselves therefrom with the help of the understanding. Let no one then be astonished that before proving the existence of body, and other necessary things, I speak of imagination of body, and of its composition. The view taken is, I repeat, immaterial, so long as we know that imagination is something indefinite, &c. As regards a true idea, we have shown that it is simple or compounded of simple ideas; that it shows how and why something is or has been made; and that its subjective effects in the soul correspond to the actual reality of its object. This conclusion is identical with the saying of the ancients, that true science proceeds from cause to effect; though the ancients, so far as I know, never formed the conception put forward here that the soul acts according to fixed laws, and is as it were an immaterial automaton. Hence, as far as is possible at the outset, we have acquired a knowledge of our understanding, and such a standard of a true idea that we need no longer fear confounding truth with falsehood and fiction. Neither shall we wonder why we understand some things which in nowise fall within the scope of the imagination, while other things are in the imagination but wholly opposed to the understanding, or others, again, which agree therewith. We now know that the operations, whereby the effects of imagination are produced, take place under other laws quite different from the laws of the understanding, and that the mind is entirely passive with regard to them. Whence we may also see how easily men may fall into grave errors through not distinguishing accurately between the imagination and the understanding; such as believing that extension must be localized, that it must be finite, that its parts are really distinct one from the other, that it is the primary and single foundation of all things, that it occupies more space at one time than at another, and other similar doctrines, all entirely opposed to truth, as we shall duly show.

Again, since words are a part of the imagination—that is, since we form many conceptions in accordance with confused arrangements of words in the memory, dependent on particular bodily conditions,—there is no doubt that words may, equally with the imagination, be the cause of many and great errors, unless we keep strictly on our guard. Moreover, words are formed according to popular fancy and intelligence, and are, therefore, signs of things as existing in the imagination, not as existing in the understanding. This is evident from the fact that to all such things as exist only in the understanding, not in the imagination, negative names are often given, such as incorporeal, infinite, &c. So, also, many conceptions really affirmative are expressed negatively, and *vice versâ,* such as uncreate, independent, infinite, immortal, &c., inasmuch as their contraries are much more easily imagined, and, therefore, occurred first to men, and usurped positive names. Many things we affirm and deny, because the nature of words allows us to do so, though the nature of things does not. While we remain unaware of this fact, we may easily mistake falsehood for truth.

Let us also beware of another great cause of confusion, which prevents the understanding from reflecting on itself. Sometimes, while making no distinction between the imagination and the intellect, we think that what we more readily imagine is clearer to us; and also we think that what we imagine we understand. Thus, we put first that which should be last: the true order of progression is reversed, and no legitimate conclusion is drawn.

Now, in order at length to pass on to the second part of this method,[31] I shall first set forth the object aimed at, and next the means for its attainment. The object aimed at is the acquisition of clear and distinct ideas, such as are produced by the pure intellect, and not by chance physical motions. In order that all ideas may be reduced to unity, we shall endeavour so to associate and arrange them that our mind may, as far as possible,

[31] The chief rule of this part is, as appears from the first part, to review all the ideas coming to us through pure intellect, so as to distinguish them from such as we imagine: the distinction will be shown through the properties of each, namely, of the imagination and of the understanding.

reflect subjectively the reality of nature, both as a
whole and as parts.

As for the first point, it is necessary (as we have
said) for our purpose that everything should be
conceived, either *solely through its essence,* or
through its proximate cause. If the thing be self-
existent, or, as is commonly said, the cause of itself, it must be understood through its essence
only; if it be not self-existent, but requires a cause
for its existence, it must be understood through its
proximate cause. For, in reality, the knowledge
of an effect is nothing else than the acquisition of
more perfect knowledge of its cause.[32] Therefore,
we may never, while we are concerned with inquiries into actual things, draw any conclusion
from abstractions; we shall be extremely careful
not to confound that which is only in the understanding with that which is in the thing itself.
The best basis for drawing a conclusion will be
either some particular affirmative essence, or a
true and legitimate definition. For the understanding cannot descend from universal axioms

[32] Observe that it is hereby manifest that we cannot
understand anything of nature without at the same time
increasing our knowledge of the first cause, or God.

by themselves to particular things, since axioms are of infinite extent, and do not determine the understanding to contemplate one particular thing more than another. Thus the true method of discovery is to form thoughts from some given definition. This process will be the more fruitful and easy in proportion as the thing given be better defined. Wherefore, the cardinal point of all this second part of method consists in the knowledge of the conditions of good definition, and the means of finding them. I will first treat of the conditions of definition.

A definition, if it is to be called perfect, must explain the inmost essence of a thing, and must take care not to substitute for this any of its properties. In order to illustrate my meaning, without taking an example which would seem to show a desire to expose other people's errors, I will choose the case of something abstract, the definition of which is of little moment. Such is a circle. If a circle be defined as a figure, such that all straight lines drawn from the centre to the circumference are equal, every one can see that such a definition does not in the least explain the essence of a circle, but solely one of its properties. Though, as I have said, this is of no importance in the case of figures and other abstractions, it is of great importance in the case of physical beings and realities: for the properties of things are not understood so long as their essences are unknown. If the latter be passed over, there is necessarily a perversion of the succession of ideas which should reflect the succession of nature, and we go far astray from our object.

In order to be free from this fault, the following rules should be observed in definition:—

I. If the thing in question be created, the definition must (as we have said) comprehend the proximate cause. For instance, a circle should, according to this rule, be defined as follows: the figure described by any line whereof one end is fixed and the other free. This definition clearly comprehends the proximate cause.

II. A conception or definition of a thing should be such that all the properties of that thing, in so far as it is considered by itself, and not in conjunction with other things, can be deduced from it, as may be seen in the definition given of a circle: for from that it clearly follows that all straight lines drawn from the centre to the circumference are equal. That this is a necessary characteristic of a definition is so clear to anyone, who reflects on the matter, that there is no need to spend time in proving it, or in showing that, owing to this second condition, every definition should be affirmative. I speak of intellectual affirmation, giving little thought to verbal affirmations which, owing to the poverty of language, must sometimes, perhaps, be expressed negatively, though the idea contained is affirmative.

The rules for the definition of an uncreated thing are as follows:—

I. The exclusion of all idea of cause—that is, the thing must not need explanation by anything outside itself.

II. When the definition of the thing has been given, there must be no room for doubt as to whether the thing exists or not.

III. It must contain, as far as the mind is concerned, no substantives which could be put into an adjectival form; in other words, the object defined must not be explained through abstractions.

IV. Lastly, though this is not absolutely necessary, it should be possible to deduce from the definition all the properties of the thing defined.

All these rules become obvious to anyone giving strict attention to the matter.

I have also stated that the best basis for drawing a conclusion is a particular affirmative essence. The more specialized the idea is, the more is it distinct, and therefore clear. Wherefore a knowledge of particular things should be sought for as diligently as possible.

As regards the order of our perceptions, and the manner in which they should be arranged and united, it is necessary that, as soon as is possible and rational, we should inquire whether there be any being (and, if so, what being), that is the cause of all things, so that its essence, represented in thought, may be the cause of all our ideas, and then our mind will to the utmost possible extent reflect nature. For it will possess, subjectively, nature's essence, order, and union. Thus we can see that it is before all things necessary for us to deduce all our ideas from physical things —that is, from real entities, proceeding, as far as may be, according to the series of causes, from one real entity to another real entity, never passing to universals and abstractions, either for the

purpose of deducing some real entity from them,
or deducing them from some real entity. Either
of these processes interrupts the true progress of
the understanding. But it must be observed that,
by the series of causes and real entities, I do not
here mean the series of particular and mutable
things, but only the series of fixed and eternal
things. It would be impossible for human in-
firmity to follow up the series of particular mutable things, both on account of their multitude,
surpassing all calculation, and on account of the
infinitely diverse circumstances surrounding one
and the same thing, any one of which may be the
cause for its existence or non-existence. Indeed,
their existence has no connection with their essence, or (as we have said already) is not an eternal truth. Neither is there any need that we should
understand their series, for the essences of particular mutable things are not to be gathered from
their series or order of existence, which would
furnish us with nothing beyond their extrinsic
denominations, their relations, or, at most, their
circumstances, all of which are very different
from their inmost essence. This inmost essence
must be sought solely from fixed and eternal

things, and from the laws, inscribed (so to speak) in those things as in their true codes, according to which all particular things take place and are arranged; nay, these mutable particular things depend so intimately and essentially (so to phrase it) upon the fixed things, that they cannot either be or be conceived without them.

Whence these fixed and eternal things, though they are themselves particular, will nevertheless, owing to their presence and power everywhere, be to us as universals, or genera of definitions of particular mutable things, and as the proximate causes of all things.

But, though this be so, there seems to be no small difficulty in arriving at the knowledge of these particular things, for to conceive them all at once would far surpass the powers of the human understanding. The arrangement whereby one thing is understood before another, as we have stated, should not be sought from their series of existence, nor from eternal things. For the latter are all by nature simultaneous. Other aids are therefore needed besides those employed for understanding eternal things and their laws; however, this is not the place to recount such aids, nor is there any need to do so, until we have acquired a sufficient knowledge of eternal things and their infallible laws, and until the nature of our senses has become plain to us.

Before betaking ourselves to seek knowledge of particular things, it will be seasonable to speak of such aids, as all tend to teach us the mode of employing our senses, and to make certain experiments under fixed rules and arrangement which may suffice to determine the object of our inquiry, so that we may therefrom infer what laws of eternal things it has been produced under, and may gain an insight into its inmost nature, as I will duly show. Here, to return to my purpose, I will only endeavour to set forth what seems necessary for enabling us to attain to knowledge of eternal things, and to define them under the conditions laid down above.

With this end, we must bear in mind what has already been stated, namely, that when the mind devotes itself to any thought, so as to examine it, and to deduce therefrom in due order all the legitimate conclusions possible, any falsehood which may lurk in the thought will be detected; but if the thought be true, the mind will readily proceed without interruption to deduce truths from it. This, I say, is necessary for our purpose, for our thoughts may be brought to a close by the absence of a foundation. If, therefore, we wish to investigate the first thing of all, it will be necessary to supply some foundation which may direct our thoughts thither. Further, since method is reflective knowledge, the foundation which must direct our thoughts can be nothing else than the knowledge of that which constitutes the reality of truth, and the knowledge of the understanding, its properties, and powers. When this has been acquired we shall possess a foundation wherefrom we can deduce our thoughts, and a path whereby the intellect, according to its capacity, may attain the knowledge of eternal things, allowance being made for the extent of the intellectual powers.

If, as I stated in the first part, it belongs to the nature of thought to form true ideas, we must here inquire what is meant by the faculties and power of the understanding. The chief part of our method is to understand as well as possible the powers of the intellect, and its nature; we are, therefore, compelled (by the considerations advanced in the second part of the method) necessarily to draw these conclusions from the definition itself of thought and understanding. But, so far, we have not got any rules for finding definitions, and, as we cannot set forth such rules without a previous knowledge of nature, that is without a definition of the understanding and its power, it follows either that the definition of the understanding must be clear in itself, or that we can understand nothing. Nevertheless this definition is not absolutely clear in itself; however, since its properties, like all things that we possess through the understanding, cannot be known clearly and distinctly, unless its nature be known previously, the definition of the understanding makes itself manifest, if we pay attention to its properties, which we know clearly and distinctly. Let us, then, enumerate here the properties of the understanding, let us examine them, and begin by discussing the instruments for research which we find innate in us.

The properties of the understanding which I have chiefly remarked, and which I clearly understand, are the following:—

I. It involves certainty—in other words, it knows that a thing exists in reality as it is reflected subjectively.

II. That it perceives certain things, or forms some ideas absolutely, some ideas from others. Thus it forms the idea of quantity absolutely, without reference to any other thoughts; but ideas of motion it only forms after taking into consideration the idea of quantity.

III. Those ideas which the understanding forms absolutely express infinity; determinate ideas are derived from other ideas. Thus in the idea of quantity, perceived by means of a cause, the quantity is determined, as when a body is perceived to be formed by the motion of a plane, a plane by the motion of a line, or, again, a line by the motion of a point. All these are perceptions which do not serve towards understanding quantity, but only towards determining it. This is proved by the fact that we conceive them as formed as it were by motion, yet this motion is not perceived unless the quantity be perceived also; we can even prolong the motion so as to form an infinite line, which we certainly could not do unless we had an idea of infinite quantity.

IV. The understanding forms positive ideas before forming negative ideas.

V. It perceives things not so much under the condition of duration as under a certain form of eternity, and in an infinite number; or rather in perceiving things it does not consider either their number or duration, whereas, in imagining them, it perceives them in a determinate number, duration, and quantity.

VI. The ideas which we form as clear and distinct, seem so to follow from the sole necessity of our nature, that they appear to depend absolutely on our sole power; with confused ideas the contrary is the case. They are often formed against our will.

VII. The mind can determine in many ways the ideas of things, which the understanding forms from other ideas: thus, for instance, in order to define the plane of an ellipse, it supposes a point adhering to a cord to be moved round two centres, or, again, it conceives an infinity of points, always in the same fixed relation to a given straight line, or a cone cut in an oblique plane, so that the angle of inclination is greater than the angle of the vertex of the cone, or in an infinity of other ways.

VIII. The more ideas express perfection of any
object, the more perfect are they themselves; for
we do not admire the architect who has planned
a chapel so much as the architect who has planned
a splendid temple.

I do not stop to consider the rest of what is
referred to thought, such as love, joy, &c. They are
nothing to our present purpose, and cannot even
be conceived unless the understanding be perceived previously. When perception is removed,
all these go with it.

False and fictitious ideas have nothing positive
about them (as we have abundantly shown),
which causes them to be called false or fictitious;
they are only considered as such through the
defectiveness of knowledge. Therefore, false and
fictitious ideas as such can teach us nothing concerning the essence of thought; this must be
sought from the positive properties just enumerated; in other words, we must lay down some
common basis from which these properties necessarily follow, so that when this is given, the properties are necessarily given also, and when it is
removed, they too vanish with it.

*   *   *   *   *   *

The rest of the treatise is wanting.